HIKER TRASH
Notes, Sketches + Other Detritus from the Appalachian Trail

HIKER TRASH

NOTES, SKETCHES + OTHER DETRITUS FROM THE APPALACHIAN TRAIL

SARAH KAIZAR
PHOTOGRAPHY BY NICHOLAS REICHARD

SKIPSTONE

Copyright © 2019 by Sarah Kaizar
All rights reserved. No part of this book may be reproduced or utilized in any form, or by any electronic, mechanical, or other means, without the prior written permission of the publisher.

Published by Skipstone, an imprint of Mountaineers Books—an independent, nonprofit publisher
Skipstone and its colophon are registered trademarks of The Mountaineers organization.
Printed in China
22 21 20 19   1 2 3 4 5

Copyeditor: Ali Shaw, Indigo
Design: Caroline Benz
Illustrations: Sarah Kaizar
Front cover illustration: Davenport shelter, Tennessee
Back cover image: Crazy Larry Hostel and proprietor with his dog (©Nicholas Reichard)
Photograph on page 15 by Sarah Kaizar
All other photographs by Nicholas Reichard and used with permission
Shelter logbook excerpts were provided by the Potomac Appalachian Trail Club and used with permission

Library of Congress Cataloging-in-Publication data is on file for this title at https://lccn.loc.gov/2019016338.

Printed on FSC®-certified materials

ISBN (hardcover): 978-1-68051-218-2

Skipstone books may be purchased for corporate, educational, or other promotional sales, and our authors are available for a wide range of events. For information on special discounts or booking an author, contact our customer service at 800.553.4453 or mbooks@mountaineersbooks.org.

Skipstone
1001 SW Klickitat Way
Suite 201
Seattle, Washington 98134
206.223.6303
www.skipstonebooks.org
www.mountaineersbooks.org

LIVE LIFE. MAKE RIPPLES.

MIX
Paper from
responsible sources
FSC
www.fsc.org   FSC® C008047

To Comrade and Switchback
For being my family in this adventure

And to Caroline
For being in every step, always

Looking south toward Rangeley (Maine)

FOREWORD

When I first set off to thru-hike and photograph the Appalachian Trail (AT) in 2015, I knew that people who were closest to me weren't exactly confident this was something I could do. Not only was I overweight, but I also didn't know a single thing about backpacking. I even grew a beard before I started my thru-hike so I could blend in and look like a real mountain man. My first night on the trail was the first time I ever set up my tent alone, and when I discovered I'd set it up backward, I thought maybe they were right to doubt me.

Not long after I began, I realized I wasn't so different from everyone else on the trail. Some sought a life-changing adventure, others had always dreamed of hiking the entire trail, and some, like me, simply wanted to create art. I wasn't sure what this journey would turn into, but I knew it would be the hardest thing I had ever done, and that's exactly what I wanted to capture. As each day passed, my confidence grew—as did my courage to shave my beard so I could once again be myself.

I photographed every day, but it wasn't the lush green mountains or the beautiful white blazes marking the trail that caught my eye. It was the people around me—they inspired me to keep going and gave me a sense of direction with my artwork. Every day I would meet someone new, each with an inspiring story and a unique trail name. I became fascinated with taking portraits of other hikers and wanted to capture their journey more than my own. The camaraderie and resiliency were unforgettable.

Months into my hike, I found myself standing on the James River Foot Bridge—but not on the path made for hikers to cross safely to the other side. A few other hikers and I were hanging over the ledge, gripping the bridge with our fingers and toes as we prepared to leap and fall forty-some-odd feet to the water below.

After we took the plunge and survived, it was all we could talk about, feeling an even deeper connection with the AT as we had joined in on an unspoken tradition among thru-hikers. We were sitting by the trail when Sarah and a few of her trail family came walking by. They mentioned also wanting to jump, but were nervous and just needed a little encouragement. It wasn't long until they too were standing on the bridge, holding on with their fingers and toes. But now I had my camera in hand and was able to capture the moment. Times like this set a foundation for new friendships formed along the trail and have now become fond memories.

When I finished my hike and stood atop Mount Katahdin, I finally understood why some may have doubted me and my willingness to keep pushing even during the hardest moments. Looking back, I realize it wasn't just my cameras that kept me going but also my friends and fellow hikers whose stories made my journey the adventure of a lifetime. I'm not sure I could have done it on my own.

Arriving home after spending over half a year in the woods was not easy, and I know I'm not alone with this feeling of being lost after completing a thru-hike. It's this wild cyclical pattern, like an addiction. You leave home to get lost in the woods, only to realize that at the end of it all, you are found. On your return home, you feel lost again. The trail was a complete metamorphosis for your life, and it isn't long thereafter that you're yearning to be back in the woods.

Before I started my hike, I'd made the decision to shoot the entire trail with analog cameras, and now here I was at home looking at over a hundred rolls of undeveloped film—my entire thru-hike condensed into a pile of canisters right in front of me. How would I find meaning in everyday life in a city when my priorities for months had been hiking, camping, meeting hikers, and photographing beauty?

The end of my thru-hike was really just the beginning. It opened my eyes to the world around me and changed who I am as an artist. When people look at my work from the AT, I want them to feel something—whether it comes from the gritty nature of shooting on film or a deep connection with the emotions displayed by the subjects. To this day, I sometimes still can't believe I hiked all 2,190 miles of the AT—in part because I still struggle when setting up my tent, but in my defense, I will always be an artist before I consider myself a mountain man, with or without the beard.

Even though Sarah and I had only a brief encounter along our hike, we share a memory that very well could be what brought us together to collaborate on this book. That's how the trail works—it brings people together who may otherwise never cross paths in the "real world."

I'm now a husband and father living in Maine. Life seems more normal these days than when I was a dirtbag on the trail, but when I look at Sarah's work, it brings me right back to my thru-hike. The rush of nostalgia gives me the same feelings I had when I saw my film being developed for the first time. It almost makes me miss my dirty pants. While the mountains tell a story of their own, I believe this book shares the trail's fascinating personality developed by those who seek freedom while walking by one blaze at a time. *Hiker Trash* is the perfect embodiment of the trail for any hiker or outdoor enthusiast who yearns to reconnect with the wild and find that feeling of being found and at home again.

— *Nicholas Reichard, 2015 thru-hiker*

Crazy Larry and his dog Sally (Damascus, Virginia)

INTRODUCTION

NO PAIN, NO RAIN, NO MAINE.
— *Appalachian Trail adage*

The Appalachian Trail (AT) is the oldest long trail in America and the longest hiking-only footpath in the world, extending 2,190 miles from Springer Mountain, Georgia, to Mount Katahdin in Maine. The trail traverses the Appalachian Mountain range, passing through fourteen states, cutting through eight national forests and two national parks, treading down the streets of small rural towns (known as "trail towns"), and crossing streams and rivers, cow pastures and farm fields, and even the backyards of a few homes.

There are many ways to experience the AT. Some hike the trail in week- or month-long sections, while others opt for short day hikes on a small portion. And each year, thousands of hikers choose to attempt the thru-hike experience, hiking consecutively from one end of the trail to the other.

A typical thru-hike of the AT can take anywhere from five to seven months to complete; the average thru-hike takes approximately six months. I started mine at Springer Mountain on March 13, 2015, and ended it barely more than six months later at Mount Katahdin on September 19.

THE TRAIL PROVIDES.

— Appalachian Trail adage

For me, the AT offered much-needed, tangible simplicity: sleep, eat, move, repeat. Thru-hiking the trail was something I had always wanted to do, but I had been content with the idea existing as an idling daydream. After the death of my father, this dream took on a stronger urgency, something that required action. I quit my job, shut down my life, and went into the woods. The decision partly fell under the heading "Life's Too Short," but more so it was an answer to the debilitating state of grief and anxiety I found myself grappling with at that time. I was desperate for a sense of relief, and having a clear, set destination was a gift. Where are you going? Maine. How are you getting there? One foot in front of the other. When are you going to get there? Whenever it happens. What are you taking with you? Only what I absolutely need.

Distance hiking forces you to function in your most exposed, vulnerable state. Over the long miles, memories I had completely forgotten—or buried—now had hours, days, weeks, months to bubble up and walk quietly with me through the trees, follow me up and down the mountains. At times, I was totally overcome by these thoughts. But my feet were on the trail, so I kept moving forward.

What I hadn't considered before beginning the AT was that these feelings would be common among the community I was hiking with. Generally, the choice to take on a thru-hike of nearly 2,200 miles is not a completely rational decision, and though many hikers I met were purely seeking adventure, others were also out there for a deeper, more personal reason. At the end of each day, I sat with other thru-hikers who were silently mulling over their own thoughts or struggles while drying their socks and boots around campfires. The comfort I found in their quiet company startled me.

HOME IS WHERE YOU HANG YOUR FOOD BAG.

— Appalachian Trail adage

Trail shelters are where you find and connect with the hiking community. When hiking the AT, these are the places where you break for lunch or spend the night, and almost always you are in the company of many other thru-hikers. The Appalachian Trail Conservancy explains shelter life this way:

There are more than 250 backcountry shelters located along the Appalachian Trail . . . for backpackers on a first-served basis. Not only are they the best places to stay dry, but they reduce hikers' impact on the Trail environment.

A typical shelter, sometimes called a "lean-to," has an overhanging roof, a wooden floor and three walls. Most (but not all) are near a creek or spring, and many have a privy nearby . . . They are an average of about 8 miles apart, but can range from 5 miles to 15 miles apart, or even as much as 30 miles apart when there is a town with some sort of lodging in between.

Trail shelters are simple structures constructed and maintained by volunteers of regional hiking clubs. They offer very basic respite from the elements but also serve as gathering places for hikers and others in the trail community as they make their way north (or south). Some thru-hikers meet only once, while others enter in to and out of each other's days for weeks, even months.

Along my thru-hike, I photographed as many trail shelters as I possibly could. Initially, I was interested in the structures themselves, since each shelter is unique, designed and constructed by the regional trail volunteers. Most are pretty utilitarian, built with rough-cut logs or stone, topped with pressed metal roofing or shakes. Others are much more elaborate, featuring multiple levels, covered porches, and skylights. The Jim and Molly Denton shelter in Warren, Virginia, even has a solar shower!

HIKE YOUR OWN HIKE.
— *Appalachian Trail adage*

When I returned home from the trail and finally sat down to put pen to paper to illustrate my journey, it was the shelters that, perhaps inevitably, took shape first. I found myself constantly pulled back to my memories of the hikers and the rotating community these shelters housed. These were the places where I found connection, and these were the people who shaped my trail experience.

I met many people on the AT seeking some sort of recalibration during a significant life transition—whether they were recently retired or divorced, newly graduated from college or high school, pursuing sobriety, or like me, seeking relief from grief. Some were working through a midlife crisis or, most commonly, dealing with a more general existential angst. One hiker nervously confessed as we were approaching the end of the trail together, "I realized I've been obsessed with finishing this thing because I assumed that I'd have everything figured out once I reached the end. Now I'm not sure if the answer is there, and I don't know what to do."

I met thru-hikers who came from Australia, Germany, Norway, and Sweden. These foreign travelers hiked the AT because they believed it was the best way to see America.

One hiker I met early on was a member of the Wounded Warrior Project, an organization serving "veterans and service members who incurred a physical or mental injury, illness, or wound while serving in the military on or after September 11, 2001." This hiker explained to me that he couldn't sleep in the community shelters because he had night terrors so severe that he worried he would unintentionally attack someone in his sleep. Another veteran on the trail warned everyone at camp to announce themselves from a distance if they were hiking behind him, because he wasn't yet able to control his reactions if startled.

I met hikers who came for the sense of adventure or simply as a way to embrace life.

I crossed paths with poets, photographers, writers, musicians, filmmakers, artists. I met a lot of software engineers.

I met hikers who had hiked the trail more than once, including a guy who was thru-hiking the AT for the sixth time. Another woman in her seventies, going by the trail name Spirit, explained that this was her third attempt to thru-hike the trail: the first time she'd contracted Lyme disease, and the second time she'd fallen and broken her hip.

A trail name, by the way, is a name you either give yourself or are given by other thru-hikers. On some level, hikers enter the trail as themselves and then, along the route, become someone new. Each person's real-world identity is checked at the door (or the trailhead), and new, alternate versions emerge.

The trail experience is often described as "the great equalizer" as everyone is moving together, generally in the same direction and with the same end goal. A trail name adds another layer to a thru-hiker's identity, as their trail self unfolds.

I WAS HAPPY IN THE MIDST OF DANGERS AND INCONVENIENCES.
— *Daniel Boone*

AT shelters each contain logbooks—damp and well-thumbed journals that convey, in a very natural and real way, not only this entangled community of hikers but also the emotions, humor, frustrations, and elations that they find out on the trail. Much of what is recorded is a "captain's log"—a day-to-day reckoning of weather and trail conditions written down by individuals as they mark their miles—as well as intimate confessions, random thoughts, drawings, reflections, and quotes.

But the logs also reveal an ongoing correspondence between hikers, providing a place to check in and record trail messages. They help keep track of trail friends and other hikers met along the way and also warn of any nearby hazards. With everyone moving at different speeds, the logs can reveal where everyone is; you can find out whether or not someone is still on the trail, or how fast you'd have to move if you wanted to catch up.

Only one trail group, the Potomac Appalachian Trail Club in Vienna, Virginia, actually archives its shelter logbooks for its region, keeping the logs on file for approximately five years before discarding them. The PATC, which generously granted me access to this archive, serves the mid-Atlantic region of the trail, so the notes from its logbooks are primarily from thru-hikers approaching the halfway point of their journey.

But what I was most drawn to were log entries that mirrored the feelings I had while hiking, or that most closely reflected the connections I made with other people. As I compiled my AT illustrations for this book, it made sense to include such logbook entries with them to offer a deeper look at life on the trail. The snippets I've excerpted here will, I hope, convey what a rich, moving experience it is to not only be so intensely immersed in nature but also find community when many need it most. In this way, I hope this book presents a collective voice—and, in this digital age, a refreshing approach, slowed down to a handwritten, hand-drawn level. The logbook entries are funny, stupid, and poignant, offering unique insight into this culture.

Hiker Trash is a collage of backpacking culture, offering a glimpse of the often offbeat, diverse community that is drawn to thru-hiking the Appalachian Trail. I wanted to share not just a personal record of my own experience but rather the elusive, visceral heart that commits thousands of people to this pilgrimage every year. My illustrations and Nicholas Reichard's wonderful photographs chase the character of the trail shelters and shelter logbooks—the heart of this work—as well as the spirit of the large community of hikers finding respite under those roofs and in those pages.

Gooch Mountain shelter, Georgia
(34.65565°, -84.04994°)

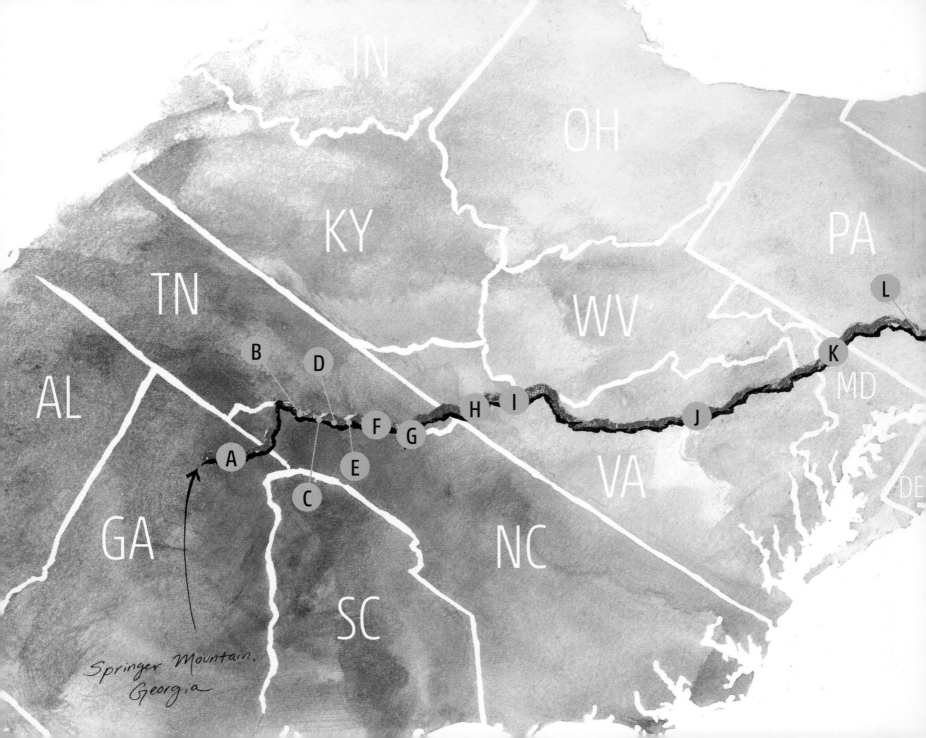

Springer Mountain,
Georgia

Mount Katahdin, Maine

ME

VT

NH

MA

CT

RI

NY

NJ

N

THE APPALACHIAN TRAIL

MAP LEGEND

A   Low Gap shelter
B   Cold Spring shelter
C   Tricorner Knob shelter
D   Davenport shelter
E   Roaring Fork shelter
F   Spring Mountain shelter
G   Overmountain shelter
H   Trimpi shelter
I   Knot Maul shelter
J   Harpers Creek shelter
K   Pine Knob shelter
L   Penn shelter
M   Kirkridge shelter
N   Mashipacong shelter
O   Fingerboard shelter
P   William Brien Memorial shelter
Q   Peru Peak shelter
R   Garfield Ridge Campsite shelter
S   Spaulding Mountain lean-to

Only shelters illustrated in *Hiker
Trash* are labeled on this map.

66 - Woke up on my 1st morning on the trail. Walked 16 miles day 1. Feeling that shit. Looking for clarity out in the woods Will settle for a nap later today.

Clarity

Comrade and rhododendrons
Cold Spring shelter, North Carolina
(35.23109°, -83.55996°)

Left: Cheesebeard, The Tailor, Van Guard, and Rabbit in the Smokies (Tennessee)
Above: Rocky Mountain High on a cold, wet day (Georgia)

I just finished hiking 14 miles ~~XXXX~~
I love hiking here in the sbenaboowah
~~XXX~~ mountains I am hiking with
my mom, dad, sister, and Dog named
Alice Alice is a portugues water
dog we just stayed at skyland we
came ~~Free~~ to ~~virginia~~ virginia from
Harvard m.a. the views are outstanding
and It's all ~~weather~~ great.

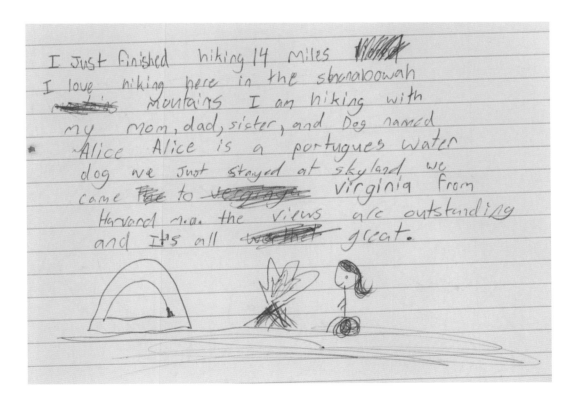

7-8 The present is naught but the past.
The future is now. El Queso Grandé

Lohner Bohner in the White Mountains (New Hampshire)

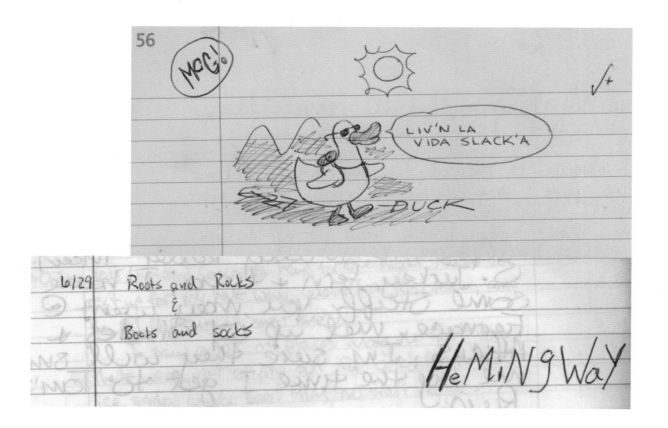

5.25

6/13 Got my first tick and saw my first bear. Also saw a snake jump out of a tree. The trail is ALIVE

-Campfire and Young Guns

Left: Thundergod at Overmountain shelter (North Carolina)
Above: Cookie Monster camping in Virginia

8/4 Saw some deer munching on grass only 10 ft away from the hut.

Kate

Switchback stretch
William Brien Memorial shelter, New York
(41.2796°, -74.0594°)

Delayed Gratification at a shelter in Virginia

5/11/15 slept with mouse, notsobad, never
made a sound...

in the nexus of space and time
here, where you are now,
is the immediate sector
of your universe
— LYNX

6/16/13 So many great + weird things today.
Loved the little rain shower that brought the
humidity down. So glad there are
segregated shelters here, Sleeping in the
"snoring" one obviously!
Apple Butter

Switchback and dappled trees
Kirkridge shelter, Pennsylvania
(40.93672°, -75.1964°)

Flick on Mount Katahdin (Maine)

22JUN15   CHOOSE A GOAL SO GREAT
YOU WILL NEVER ACHIEVE IT
UNTIL YOU BECOME THE PERSON
WHO CAN.   — TABASCO

Big, small
Spring Mountain shelter, Tennessee
(35.95177°, -82.79007°)

6/25 "I think all my friends think I'm the 'Hills are Alive'n' it every fucking day. When in Reality I'm hiking through a tunnel trying not to get stung by wasps when I'm shitting" —John Wayne
    I think we're over Virginia...
                        xoxo Juke + Wayne

6/27
C Caesar
It's been a cool day for hicking

6/27
Rainman reproduces asexually.

6/7   GO GO GO!
                        —North Star

9/20 Pardon my expression, but FUCK anxiety. Staying out of town for a while man. NO idea what I'd do without you Mother Nature♥
                        ♡♡♡ Breosy

8/10/15   Do you ever wonder what people say about you after they meet you?
NoBo
Thru-Hiker   —HOMIE

5/18 Completely wiped... but I am here. Grandma Bear

6/16 I am literally sweating sugar
♡ Willy Wonka

7/25 SOBO can be so lonely!! Making new friends only to never see them again. But it's okay--I have a LOT of thinking & soul-searching to accomplish in the next ~2 1/2 months. Just hoping that Pacman can figure out what's going on with his ankle & correct it. Resupply in Front Royal tomorrow.
         xo GrossBaby & Pacman xo X X
         xo   xo
\SOBO Pa-Ga xo xo
   "Don't get sucked into an
American Dream Ponzi scheme that
  was never intended to include you". —

7/25 | our universes are running in mirrored directions. I pause here where you did. Headed North where you looked South. Light years

— MacGuyver

Trail family
Pine Knob shelter, Maryland
(39.54249°, -77.60181°)

6/6 Rained like crazy last night. Need longer sleeping pad. Hopefully taking a shower today at the state park. Life is great!

"Life is 10% what happens to you and 90% how you react to it."
— Charles Swindoll

— Dirty Rotten Liar
AKA The Artist Formerly Known As
Papa John / Jizzy J / Chonks / Chanda

Right: Gingah T at a shelter in Virginia
Far right: Shelter life in Vermont

7/27 Stopped in for some grub, pumped to keep climbing the mountain. Happy Hiking ya crazies and remember "It's NOT THE MOUNTAIN WE CONQUER, BUT OURSELVES"

P.S. Thanks for the oreos! They were delicious!

-3 fast guys in the woods now Fox and Cotton

Left: Pie and Earth at Curley Maple Gap shelter (Tennessee)
Above: Banjo Black's dog at Curley Maple Gap shelter (Tennessee)

7/6 How did I get here?
   Where the HELL Am I?
   →Theseus
7/v I DON'T CARE HOW THESEUS GOT HERE, I'M JUST GLAD HE DID
WHEN I WAS HERE. -RABBIT

Foot rub
Peru Peak shelter, Vermont
(43.3012°, -72.95184°)

Flagstaff Lake (Maine)

618 | Watch the hole behind the fire-pit! There is a big Copperhead!
-Steam Machine

14 Jun 2015 Wilderness in for the night. All ready for the firefly show. A fearless deer just walked right through the middle of camp!

6/6: Today, we get to shower... it's the little things. :)
— Ariel Hicks Aka *Spicy*

July 5, 2014
Twenty-three miles, Ten deer, Four bear, a fellowship of three, two broken tent poles, and one heck of a day!
— Scout, Flipper, WoW

Clearity at a shelter in Pennsylvania

8/8/2015 Life Rules! Keep on Walking in the tree
World.   ~Hurculeas

Trekking pole lineup at Mountaineer Falls shelter (Tennessee)

8/22/14

Stayed the night + spent most of yesterday afternoon here. Now waiting for the rain to clear.(23:14)

We Really enjoyed staying in such a beautiful + clean shelter. Big thanks to the overseers.

Lavender + OL'MAN RIVER

7/4 I was the only person here last night. Took my damn time this morning — It's been lovely. Happy B-day, America! - Firefly

Left: Lunch break
Spaulding Mountain lean-to, Maine
(44.99577°, -70.34134°)

6-22 Okay, so I ended up staying the night... But now I'm going into town today... PROMISE!

✱ 9

P.S. Someone check on those 2 blue tents tonight if they're still there. There's been no movement... could be zombies over there. Or maybe they're shiners... just out checking on their stash. Or maybe there's a scared little animal in there in need of a hug! So.... someone go check on that.

Left: Voldemort and Burnout at Wilson Valley lean-to in the 100-Mile Wilderness (Maine)
Above: Pie and Kiwi cooking dinner at Overmountain shelter (North Carolina)

Interlude in the White Mountains (New Hampshire)

7/3 | HEY DIXIE + REBEL, WHAT DID THE BIG TOMATO SAY
TO THE LITTLE TOMATO WHO COULDN'T KEEP UP???
"KETCHUP"
    NOW "CATCH UP" SO WE CAN CROSS
THE 1/2 WAY POINT TOGETHER!
                        —LAND MAMMAL

7/13 | SOMEDAY I VOW TO LEAVE CAMP BEFORE NOON..
                        Ryan

8/14 Saw 7 bears on my way to this hut. They seem
to be everywhere in the Shenandoah. The trek from
Pass Mt hut to here is not an easy one. We
got lost three different times - don't take the horses
trail. 4 miles to the next wayside. NO FLYING RATS!
    - Scuba Steve.

I am Julia, and bears are scary...

UNIT ONE   ♡ Julia (age 14)
UNIT FUN   (Gucci Avocado)

20th May '14 Pancake + BabyFace — still alive and still on the trail.
Just had lunch in town and a tough 2.5 miles...
Did you know? Bear cubs stumble when they run
and they are so fluffy!

Left: Earth journals at a shelter in Tennessee
Above: Cookie Monster at annual Trail Days in Damascus, Virginia

5/27. Woke up to a symphony of birds and a smile on my face ☺ I think my cold is on its way out. Huzzah!
    - Vulture.
 · P.S. - HEY RUSH!! HEY YELLOW BIRD!!

Snack share in the rain
Mashipacong shelter, New Jersey
(41.25216°, -74.68594°)

5/28 There's a miliped stalking you. Everywhere you turn there he is.
- Eternal Scout

Murder that bug

Trail Devil

7/3 Berber Stemps her! Crazy misadventures. Phone gone, so that sucks. But just when I thought that people were inherently evil, so many crazy but wonderful acts of kindness happened to me that my faith is restored in humanity! Blah I'm tired. TOO many emotions. (oh and I was up and out the tent around 4am......)
Baby Steps

6/6 Snakes stopping by for lunch!

DON'T KILL THE SNAKE THAT
LIVES IN THE RAFTER!
IT EATS THE MICE!!

Pie and Cheesebeard play Magic at 501 shelter (Pennsylvania)

15 Jun 2015 Wilderness in for the night. Praying for my food. May the raccoons and flying squirrels (?) and other critters stay far away. Saw a baby bear cub wander through down below by the spring; though no sign of Mama bear. Thank you hiking/camping Gods!

AND NOW for the Question of The Day (QOTD)

Would you rather eat noodle sides for dinner the rest of your life or walk through spider's webs every morning the rest of your life?   Eat spider webs.

XOXO - Wilderness

P.S. In case you were wondering, YES, exploding blisters do indeed hurt like a M-fucker while hiking.

6/1   Fuck, where is Harper's Ferry?

6/2   I don't really want to hike in   - John Seto
the Rain, but hell what choice
do I have.

HOT SAUCE

3/25   I was once paid to put bullets through peoples foreheads. Today I walk in the open carrying only a pack and no weapon. The forest helps me heal.
      Sgt. Gilbert + Sgt Mollohan 3/1 Marines

Lord, remind me of how brief my time on earth will be. Remind me that my days are numbered - how fleeting my life is. You have made my life no longer than the width of my hand. My entire lifetime is just a moment to you; at best, each of us is but a breath.
      Psalm 39: 4-5
       ~Dragon Fly

Left: Cold, cold break
Roaring Fork shelter, North Carolina
(35.805°, -82.94978°)

Bear Finder crossing one of the many streams in the 100-Mile Wilderness (Maine)

5/27 - Jolly Rancher passing
through; psyching myself up
for the (dreaded) roller coaster...

7-15   It was alot of fun doing insane miles.
But I realised we are half way.
So I don't care if I finish last.
Time to really enjoy each day and
push this hike till 10/15. 13 miles
a day and an entire extra month
on trail sounds nice. —Gasket

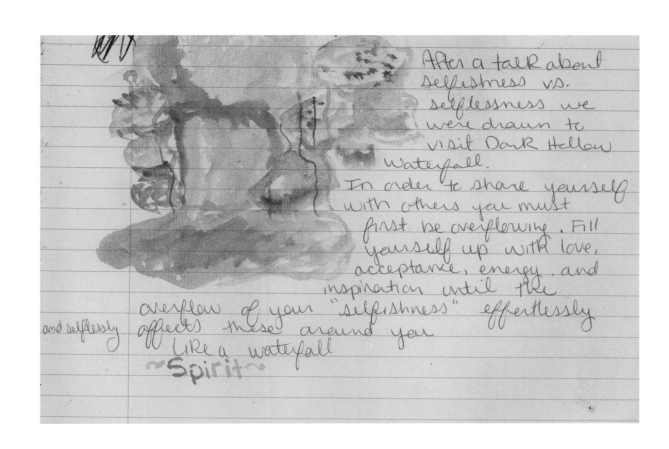

After a talk about selfishness vs. selflessness we were drawn to visit Dark Hollow Waterfall.

In order to share yourself with others you must first be overflowing. Fill yourself up with love, acceptance, energy, and inspiration until the overflow of your "selfishness" effortlessly *and selflessly* affects those around you like a waterfall

~Spirit~

6/23/16 Pokey and Lupine here. We met at school in this beautiful state, and currently live in Colorado. Hiking the AT was something we always wanted to do, and after two years of saving and planning, here we are (almost) halfway there. Not sure exactly what we were expecting to get out of this, other than the journey of a lifetime. So far it has been.

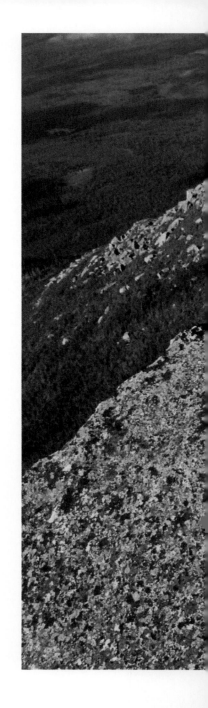

Ascending Mount Katahdin, the steepest section of the Appalachian Trail (Maine)

Knock and Honeybuns celebrating the end of a half-year adventure atop Mount Katahdin (Maine)

6/8 To those who have made it thus far:
Congrats! you're just under the half way point.
- keep going strong - PA is a boot buster but stay optimistic.
- Chris & Kate

love it!
Thank you.
(x2!)

6/9 Nice shelter. Lousy weather. TRONCHEF

Everything Was
Beautiful
And
Nothing
Hurt

→ Vonnegut! of?

- IHHBA
5/30/16

6-19-15 Shenandoah Park,
Where the deer were once extinct,
But now roam freely
— A haiku by SQUAREPEG

While we hike, we have time to think,
Time for introspection and meditation.
We have time to examine our lives
and ponder the course we will chart from here.
We are a product of our actions past and
our future potential.
Now is the time to know yourself and
find out who you truely are.
SQUAREPEG's random thoughts.

Blaze
William Penn shelter, Pennsylvania
(40.49559°, -76.41409°)

N.B. DO NOT TRUST BEAR POLE
Lower one has been hit
multi nights in a row

4/30 DO NOT HANG FOOD
BEHIND SHELTER

There is a flying squirrel (or something)
problem. Try the hanger near the privy.
The fuckers ate my Sea-to-Summit
♥ Cap't tying knots

Bear bag lines, Hawk Mountain shelter (Georgia)

06/01/05 0622 I have a tent for two, but it's awful lonely just spooning with my Pack.
— Weedeat 🙂

Comrade in the cold
Tricorner Knob shelter, North Carolina
(35.69375°, -83.25653°)

7/18/14 Had a great & restful night here. Enjoyed sleeping in the rain storm. Headed to Front Royal.

— Four Leaf, Valet & Ella

Right: Pony Puncher and Food Truck at Gentian Pond shelter (New Hampshire)
Far right: Sparkles and Peg Leg at Stratton Pond, Vermont

Smoke break after crossing Lehigh Gap (Pennsylvania)

5-13 Rough night in deer lick, loud group and creepy noises, still trying to adjust to the whole middle of nowhere thing. All that caused a late start and a bad nights sleep. Beautiful shelter... wish we could stay here, but off we go

Twiggy

Bear guard
Davenport shelter, Tennessee
(35.7693°, -83.1234°)

Heading back to the trail after a night with trail legend Bob Peoples (Tennessee)

6/23 Finally got a trail name. Fell down a switch back and when I got up I yelled "short cut" so my trail name is now short cut.
— Takoda — Short cut.

06/17/15 So, yeah... Just standing in the woods, by the side of the road, filling up my water in the spring, and trying not to look like a crazy person out in the woods.
— Weedeater

8 Paws outside the Lakes of the Clouds hut near Mount Washington (New Hampshire)

7/7/15 So surreal being back in my backyard; really feels good seeing some familiar trail. Around 5 years ago my brother and I section hiked the SNP, been having some great memories moving thru the park. Took a zero at Bearfence yesterday as it is my favorite mountain in the Shenandoahs. Loving life today and very grateful for this beautiful weather!

Woodfoot

9/6 LITTLE OVER A YEAR SINCE OUR THRU-HIKE, WE WERE NEARBY AND HAD TO TOUCH THE TRAIL AGAIN - FEELS LIKE COMING HOME! WE'LL SIGN OUR OLD TRAIL NAME, EVEN THOUGH IT NO LONGER IS ACCURATE, OUR GA WEDDING WAS OUR ULTIMATE FINISH TO OUR TRAIL EXPERIENCE! BEST TO ALL THOSE WHO CAME BEFORE AND AFTER US!
'THE NEARLY-WEDS'

Bad day
Fingerboard shelter, New York
(41.26327°, -74.10399°)

5/22/15 After spending last night zombie walking and this morning like a vampire stuck in a coffin hidding from the sun it feels good to relax with sun on my shoulders.
           - Eternal Scout   Hi Obi Wan!
                              Hi Vortex!

Everyone is out here to hike, so how can they do that if they are still sleeping? Go ahead and wake everyone up.

                                        Trail Devil

5/22 I want a do over! After a week of beautiful

Laces at Zealand Falls hut (New Hampshire)

6/11   I AM 'NEITHER A REAL DOCTOR NOR A REAL PICKLE — DR. PICKLES

/11 Day after a big rain + all is bliss. The streams
are running, sky is blue, air is cool + breezy...
the first fall day. Top it off as a nice
mid-morning break at this awesome shelter.
I love the huge tree where it fell just to
the right of the shelter. I've heard that
a tree takes as long to fully decay into
the soil as it takes to grow.
    SOBO   MEGA→
        -1Step

5/22. **AMAZED** + overjoyed to see Birk tonight when I rolled up to the shelter. The trail creates good friendships. I got so cold last night that I bought a $25 HEAVY blanket at Big Meadow today. OUCH! But I'm so cozy that I don't regret it.

Five.

Early days, shelter crowd
Low Gap shelter, Georgia
(34.77624°, –83.8245°)

Pyro's dog staying warm by the fire at Curley Maple Gap shelter (Tennessee)

5/14 Cap'n Kirk· Beautiful day to hike! In for the night. Already saw 3 mice. These buggers are not shy. Better not fight me tonight... I'll lose cause I always back down. Gosh I wish I could stand up to mice. They just are ferocious Idk if I spelled that right. Oh well... I don't know why I'm writing so much. Maybe I'm dehydrated & getting crazy... guess you have to be crazy to walk a 1000 miles... BooM! I'll stop now. Also, I need a life.

⤷ Loving found 4 in his bag this morning ewn!

Beartooth
ALSO Aggressive/birthing/relentless mice! BEWARE

I wish my fingers were warm enough to doodle but this is all I've got:

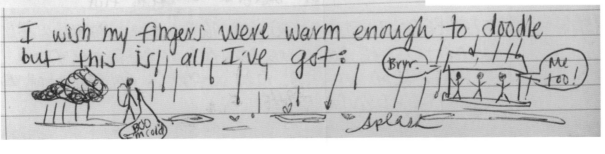

7/6   In @ about 6:00 p.m. Man, it seems like I was passing the quarter way point just the other day. I've been avoiding thinking about the end because it seemed so far away. Now when the thought creeps into my mind, I get kind of an anxious/nervous feeling. ¨

— Juice

Above: Car Bomb relaxes with a book at Overmountain shelter (North Carolina)
Right: Pie and Blad on a zero day in Pearisburg, Virginia

6/19 Really rough morning. Seem to have
all the symptoms of Lime disease...
Feeling much better later in the day.
May head into town w/ half brew to
get checked out & put some ease to
my troubled mind. If it isnt one thing
its another -- so much for a 40 mile
day... still have the Ⓐ doe.
ΔΔ -LINK
ΔΔ I have put in a Order
for...

Met a bunch of cool people here. gonna try to stop rushing and worrying out here and just enjoy it. Staying a month in Duncannon I lost my hiker legs but worrying wont make them come back any quicker.

one last

6/8   THINGS I ENJOY: DRY SOCKS, DRY BOOTS, DRY TARP, BACON

THINGS I DONT ENJOY: DRY COUNTIES

                                    - OG MILES

Poppins is back in action; I have some rediculous knee high compression socks that, I'm rocking, and anti-biotics to prevent an infection in my foot due to the impacted blister. I am glad to be back in the woods, it was actually quite boring & depressing at home for a few days. going to enjoy a couple of chill days before tackling the 4 state challenge that is right up the trail.
P.S. This shelter is wonderful!

                    - Poppins

9/26·2014 So ends the SOBO journey of
Tin Can. Must flip flop back to Harpers Ferry.
Contracted a lung infection from another hiker
who should remain anonymous (Turtle), also left
knee in bad shape, shoulder still painfull from
50 ft tumble @ Rock Maze S. of Boiling Springs PA.
       Hiking Gear (boots, back pack) seem to need repair
almost daily. Springer Mtn. GA. was ultimate goal,
Shenandoah N.P. secondary. Well could've been worse.
   To all who read this, Happy Trails, don't give up
on your dreams, and remember it's not an adventure
until something goes wrong. Love, peace to all
   NOBO I go.   "—Tin Can Dan"

       One more thing, "A journey of a thousand miles
begins with the first step" So, take that first step
I will return.   "Tin Can" Dan Updegrove out

7/18 | THINGS THAT MOTIVATE ME TO
         HIKE FASTER |
   1. THUNDER   ✓
   2. RAIN   ✓
   3. ICE CREAM   ✓
   4. BED   ✓

GOTTA KEEP MOVIN. "FOR THE LOVE OF
— Brave Heart   GOD, JUST KEEP
                          HIKING !!!!"

Sun, shade
Knot Maul shelter, Virginia
(37.0008°, −81.40446°)

5/7   JOHNNY CASH STEPPED OUT OF THE RING OF FIRE HERE.

6-16

What's it all about?

A long walk, A life changer! Never be the same. Share the love! Frosty

Above: Hiking along Franconia Ridge, above treeline once more (New Hampshire)
Right: On South Twin Mountain, SOBOs and NOBOs share insights about the way ahead (New Hampshire)

7/17 KStar here. Lots of feelings!
Jeni + Atlas — Hope you had a restful stay at
the hostel. Thinking of you a lot. The trail fam
wishes you well, and hopes to cross paths soon. ♡

Passing through
Overmountain shelter, North Carolina
(36.12348°, -82.05428°)

Rusty at the Lakes of the Clouds hut (New Hampshire)

Clover at Delaware Water Gap on the New Jersey–Pennsylvania border

7/1 The Appalachian Trail is a relentless teacher. Everything works out in the end; if it hasn't worked out, it's not the end.
— Twiggs · P.

7/10 Started April 16th from Amicalola Falls and took two weeks off from May 19th – June 3rd. I would have to say that throughout my adventure so far, I've come to realize that many people always come to the trail, thinking of it as recreation or a space that is there for them and others to share. However, if you walk this trail long enough you really start to feel and understand that the trail calls out to you and everyone else out here. And if you are willing to listen and change who you are, then the trail will really shape + mold you into the best version of you, you can be. — Jefe

7/16/16 The miles beat me senseless. The mind-melting views, friendships, and wildlife spoil me rotten. It's a complicated relationship, a thru-hike, but I'm in love with it every day.
♡ (Firebird, ATX, started April 10)

North Carolina ridge camp with Comrade, Wookie, Gump, and Hula Hoop

Cliffhanger listening to stories from legendary thru-hiker Lohner Bohner

6/26 The trail for me was meant to be a personal challenge — to understand that the only creature strong enough to undermine what I do — is myself.

It is my transition — progress into allowing myself to feel — wether it'd be nervous or anxious — without fearing. Allowing and accepting, loving and caring for my mind and body — to better care for myself so that I can tackle the next challenges coming my way. ♡

Kaleidoscope
Quito - Ecuador
Boston - Mass ♥

dia a dia

Celebrating during Trail Days in Damascus, Virginia

7/21 last shelter log entry for a long time.
This has been the adventure of a
lifetime! I'm so happy that I found
the AT, because it has changed my
life! Then I'd to like do say Thanks
To The degenerates, rumbles & especially
Legs & Color Bandit.
Thank you All of you are
great people. OVER→

ACKNOWLEDGMENTS

I'm deeply grateful to my editors, Kate Rogers and Mary Metz, and the team at Mountaineers Books for taking a chance on this project, pushing me to make this work stronger, and ultimately making this happen. Thank you.

Thank you to Nicholas Reichard for contributing your excellent photographs to this book. Your sensitivity in capturing these moments on the trail is so on point; I'm so grateful to include your work in this project.

Thank you to my sister Caroline Benz for creating the beautiful layout work and cover design for this book, sorting through and gracefully making sense of a lot of different pieces. I love you, Caroface.

Thank you to my parents, Kathie and John Melsky, and my sister Schyler Melsky for rooting for me on trail and off, always. Love to the entire O'Neill gang for supporting me and my work in all the places, at all the things, all the time.

Thank you to John Kaizar for joining me on this and so many other adventures. Big thanks to the entire Kaizar family for watching Petey, sending supplies, making cookies, and all forms of cheerleading in between.

I'm honestly not sure I would have made it through the hike without the support of my trail family. Thank you to Markie Rexroat for your perspective, humor, and mountaintop delirium. Thanks also to Todd and Brandi Yates for every pause on the hike required to take another damn shelter picture. Thanks to all of you for sharing your journals, photos, and other notes from the trail while I was working on this project.

I'm lucky and grateful to have so many amazing friends in my life, and I want to thank all of you for helping me think through this work and for your ongoing support. At the risk of leaving someone out, I want to send a few extra thanks to Shelly Petcaugh, Lauren Netti, Alison Filla, the Harrison family, Therese Madden, Jessica Kourkounis, Julie and Rob Siglin, and Matt Waters. Special high fives to those who also came out for a jaunt on the trail! Mark O'Neill (so. many. rocks.), Rich Baniewicz (Duncannon!), Shao Ma, and Candace Wong.

Love and thanks to Sean Kelley for your friendship, encouragement, and one-hour rule.

Thank you to my favorite small but mighty businesses in Bristol Borough—Calm Waters Coffee Roasters and Noble Earth—for hosting me in your spaces while I was sketching, writing and thinking out loud. Special thanks to the crew at Philosotea (my philosopeeps!), with an extra shout-out to Gary Alloway and Scotty Meiser for your friendship and support.

Thank you to the Appalachian Trail Conservancy for making this entire experience possible.

photo David Slaten

ABOUT THE AUTHOR

Sarah Kaizar is an illustrator and designer living and working in Philadelphia. Sarah holds a BFA from Tyler School of Art, Temple University, and she has shown her work in galleries and museums in and around the Philadelphia area, including 3rd Street Gallery, The Delaware Contemporary, The Schuylkill Center for Environmental Education, and the Woodmere Art Museum.

See more of Sarah's work at www.sarahkaizar.com.

ABOUT THE PHOTOGRAPHER

Nicholas Reichard is a photographer and filmmaker who lives in Biddeford, Maine.

Learn more at www.nicholasreichard.com.

SKIPSTONE is an imprint of independent, nonprofit publisher Mountaineers Books. It features thematically related titles that promote a deeper connection to our natural world through sustainable practice and backyard activism. Our readers live smart, play well, and typically engage with the community around them. Skipstone guides explore healthy lifestyles and how an outdoor life relates to the well-being of our planet, as well as of our own neighborhoods. Sustainable foods and gardens; healthful living; realistic and doable conservation at home; modern aspirations for community—Skipstone tries to address such topics in ways that emphasize active living, local and grassroots practices, and a small footprint.

Our hope is that Skipstone books will inspire you to effect change without losing your sense of humor, to celebrate the freedom and generosity of a life outdoors, and to move forward with gentle leaps or breathtaking bounds.

All of our publications, as part of our 501(c)(3) nonprofit program, are made possible through the generosity of donors and through sales of more than 800 titles on outdoor recreation, sustainable lifestyle, and conservation. To donate, purchase books, or learn more, visit us online:

www.skipstonebooks.org
www.mountaineersbooks.org

ALSO AVAILABLE: